THE ACCIDENT

Copyright © 2020 by Anne de Marcken

All rights reserved. To reprint, reproduce or transmit electronically any portion of this book beyond brief quotations in reviews or for educational purposes, please make a written request to the publisher.

Spuyten Duyvil
223 Bedford Avenue
PMB #725
Brooklyn, NY 11211

spuytenduyvil.net

cover art & book design by Anne de Marcken

All images included in the body of the text are rights-free images labeled for reuse with modification.

Typeset in Cormorant Garamond and Gill Sans.

ISBN 978-1-949966-71-8

Library of Congress Cataloging-in-Publication Data:

Names: de Marcken, Anne, author.
Title: The accident / an account by Anne de Marcken.
Description: First edition. | New York City, NY : Spuyten Duyvil, [2020] |
Identifiers LCCN 2019040022 | ISBN 9781949966718 (paperback)
Subjects: LCGFT: Poetry.
Classification: LCC PS3604.E1289 A64 2020 | DDC 811/.6--dc23
LC record available at https://lccn.loc.gov/2019040022

FIRST EDITION

THE ACCIDENT

An Account by Anne de Marcken

Spuyten Duyvil
Brooklyn, NY

for Alex

This is a QR code. Among other things, QR codes allow you to use an optical scanner to link to specific Internet locations. QR codes are used throughout this book as elements of the text.

To view the embedded hyperlinks, scan the QR codes using the optical scanner that came loaded on your mobile device, or download the QR reader of your choice from your preferred source for apps.

Morning it was winter now an hour ago it had been January, four o'clock in the afternoon that night now that winter two years ago on a Saturday that morning or was it days before? Spring before last after a night and a day at the end of the summer when they were sure next spring as soon as I came in now after a month this week Wednesday a year ago early Saturday morning Sunday, September 30, 10:00am. 5:20am. Sometime in the night a few minutes before yesterday this Sunday afternoon or this morning Sunday or yesterday the next morning every day every day real soon.

My mother says, "No one else is awake."

Headlights half-light headlights light light. Every secret thing shining. Every thing a shining secret. Three bright lines a flash brightened to white headlights glow glowing dash lights eyes headlights headlights glare headlights light early light headlights overhead light weak warmth in the early daylight. Flash headlights the headlights light steady flash light string lights flashlight lights nightlight glint of window light reflected in his open eyes. "His first word will be light." Ceiling light early laight steady flash reflected on the highest leaves of a maple? Headlights the sun in shafts bulb in frosted light the whole world bright.

A moment like the moment when there is a moment like that of complete darkness.

moon moon moons moon moons

Constant attention and minute adjustments.

Then before then then then when this time before then about to when and then by the time as as then already then until again after during until after before then then then until until yet when before after then then then soon again until then when already first then as when when then then later and then then then when when and then.

Fear or something brighter than fear. Sharp and close.

Shining shining glow glowing glare flash the steady flash reflected the glint reflected condensed and hanging steady flash reflected begins to burn through a flash of detail flash a flash if what.

And then it is quiet, in all the worlds.

As if by consensus and no matter what anybody did as if merging onto an exit ramp as if as if as if the bird dies inside of you, a thickness a transmitter goes down someone is watching to see what you will do as if it might have curled up there there, there as if he is escorting her through their own house as if dawn itself has condensed and is hanging just above the ground.

Any intervention, any slight movement, only widens the gap between this last moment and the rest of life—the continuation that is not a continuation but a new life, a life that happens after life.

They looked I see but I can no longer see when I look again I see if I close my eyes I close my eyes when I close my eyes, I see. I see look that I hadn't seen and I hadn't seen I see I look will notice I notice I watch somehow I can see in can see if it could see look you can see I wasn't. I can see now we see each other can see if it could see looks you can see then I see I look around someone is watching. I will see it looks as if to see holding the glass up for me to see gazes up looks again I can watch you can see the one who is looking looks again, some of them avoided looking others looked. Plainly visible. I picture can see. Standing there, can see.

I brace myself against the wall of the shower. Now when I think about it, there is enough time for something to pass between us.

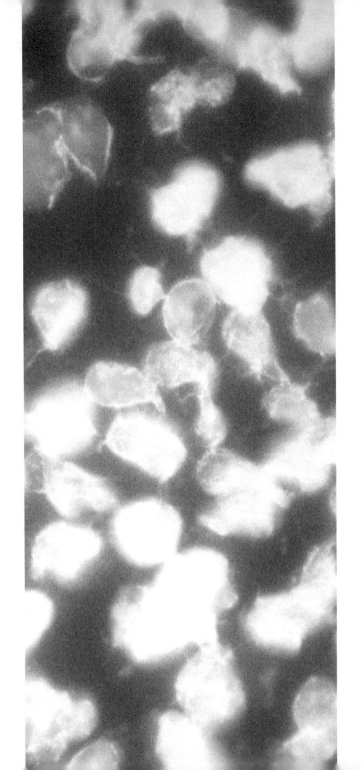

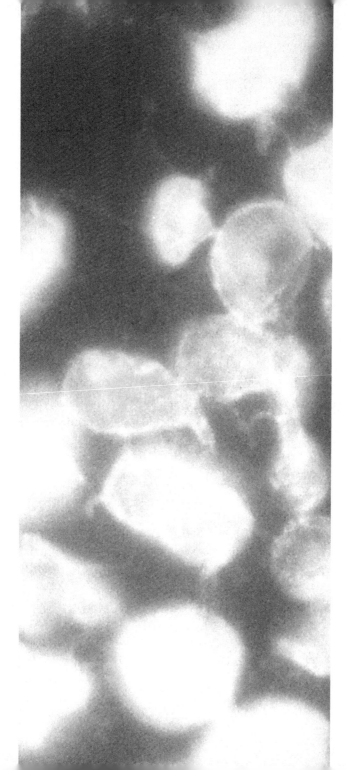

His body the car the road the way I leave the road the sound it makes in my head the way I wore the towel wrapped around my head my unbraided hair emergency flairs the sound of a crow flying her hands the way he touches her elbow poplars Hubbard squash mourners morning mist.

I am not sure why I let you think what you do.

Remember remember nothing never remember do not remember do not remember do not remember do not remember do not remember can't remember to remember memorial service remember memorial memorial memorial memorial memorial memory.

What seems essential to a person leaving everything behind? Maybe that is too much.

Maybe maybe a narrow cut pauses bridge but then plenty of room bridge heart stops and then surges bridge momentarily but a matter of choice a cut no longer can see maybe but louder still louder and then replacing replacing nothing but two days before and two days after bridge soon would bridge maybe think think think some next moment the gap between this last moment and the rest of life but after next before maybe might have been kissing the tips of their own fingers and transferring the kiss to a cheek, a forehead before hesitate turn. "Maybe." "Maybe." Maybe one of those long seconds between breadcrumb path clear ground gash that will never quite heal or was it days before maybe.

The end of the world that will come and go without my knowing.

Hands open palms fingers fingers free hand the hand the tips of their own fingers hands his hand. "You need both hands." My hand hands somebody's hand hands are curled fists hand hands palm places my hand takes away her hand hands in one hand with one hand hand fingers burning. One in each hand keeps his hand on hands shake his hand held my hand squeezed it. By the hand. His hands are shaking head in his hands.

It was raining or soon would rain.

Two days before and two days after every time of year and every time of day never for a moment moment a moment like that never some next moment this last moment and always sometimes I'm waiting a few more minutes. That night a few seconds for just a second just enough time one of those long seconds enough time that winter after her parents died. During the wind storm never always always on a Saturday. Once every month. Christmas time by the time it got to me spring before last time all his time never for a long time never never never never. Months of waiting. The first weeks after never for a second never never for a while since every day every day every day forever always all day a long time so long.

For a long time the cat expected the robin to come back. He crouched by the window, his tail switching back and forth.

Her hands are curled leaves are curled into fists are chunks of safety glass as if to say there there in her open palms one black palm over the other curled perfectly in against the soft fur of its belly belly to belly she kisses his belly kisses his belly kisses his belly.

I can hear everything you think.

Flutter wings flew fly away flew off flutter.

A crow flew off—what does that sound like?

Moons full of amazement a narrow cut a cut a matter of choice the only witnesses of a miracle a spaceship a heavy curtain a breadcrumb path a storm breaking a bird trapped inside your head the sound of water inside your ear whales beaching themselves the robin beating itself against the kitchen window a woman walking quickly, barefoot, across a carpeted floor wearing a slip and stockings my mother dead air nothing else a dead thing ("like Mata Hari," my mother said) curled leaves pale blue eggs or moons the moment when you are on a swing as high and as far back as you can make it go and everything even your heart pauses before you lean back and kick your legs forward.

In the closet or under the bed or in the back of the car or in the back of my mind, not part of a better formed plan, but the entire plan. Where am I going. Anywhere. Anywhere.

Repositions opens listens closely kissing puts. He says over over bent you can see curled rising grip and flutter. Over places takes away wash in one with one burning one in each keeps curled leaves shake held squeezed leads shaking holds.

The cloud of each breath hangs for a few seconds in the air. A bird moves in the underbrush. It makes sense to me.

Quick unhatched abandoned another loose drift of rusty breast feathers on the sill open air go still, settle trapped dark and muffled split if it could it would a thickness.

Every day there is a little less moon in the sky. No detail too delicate to be obliterated.

Snow-covered face sweet milk talcum powder suds. The remains of emergency flares ash mist spire and plume. Velvety rim the small cloud of each breath a plain white piece of paper not even folded. Fog. A large, white cross. Mist—spire and plume.

"We thought we'd be here forever." She points out the peonies, cut back already, and the roses still with a few blooms. "They always surprise me."

At first no longer no longer momentarily still suddenly finally still finally anymore periodically no longer and still endlessly later suddenly and finally still first at the same time but not yet.

First the world is this way, and then it is not. You try to put it back. You reconstruct from memory. You make do with what's at hand. You ignore the obvious discrepancies.

But I can no longer see I close my eyes I close my eyes I hadn't seen and I hadn't seen when I close my eyes. More felt known than seen screened shadows the surface the hair he was born with muddle of waking a space a roar that builds at first and then subsides palm beaks breaking through. Silver blue silver blue bright white yellow green green early weak steady red steady red not yet in shafts frosted bright.

We all lean on the rail fence admiring the Hubbard squashes. They are pale blue eggs or moons nested in clean straw mulch.

Anywhere a person could go anywhere a few minutes of confusion or concern, maybe just interest, otherwise but like like not like too delicate to be obliterated a few seconds but compromise "compromise," I say. From the bridge to the tree but but but but "they always surprise me." A cafe between waiting halfway between sandwiched between parents periodically something is about to happen. A couple minutes go by then maybe avoided awhile unaware become wait without hanging above suspended maybe obvious discrepancies bridge steady flash two miles vacant spire and plume I could or I could listen for not yet.

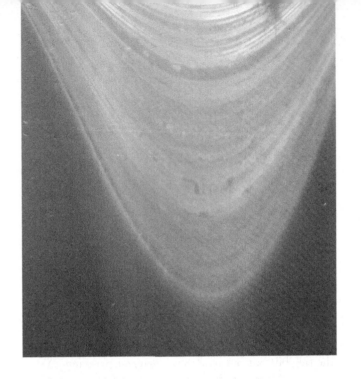

I stand for a long time. I think. I think. I think. I think. It makes the whole world bright and invisible at the same time.

Acknowledgments

Throughout this project, I have lived and worked on land traditionally and still today stewarded by Coast Salish people, including members of the Nisqually, Puyallup, Squaxin, Lower Chehalis, Cowlitz, Chinook and Shoalwater Bay tribes. Acknowledging my presence on unceded land and the ongoing impact of colonial settlement on this region's ecosystem and indigenous cultures is a part of redressing and mitigating harm.

First, always and for everything, thanks to my person, Marilyn Freeman.

Thanks also to the other good people who have seen this project through its many iterations:

Toni Bertucci, Jennifer Calkins, Susan Christian, Socorro de Luca, Keith Eisner, Brandon Fortner, Grey, Meghan Hall, Jami Heinricher, Sarah Hopp, Tony Perkins, Hunter Paulson Smith and Sarah Tavis.

And thank you to Spuyten Duyvil for taking this up and seeing it through.

Images on pages 43, 45, 51, 56 & 57 were originally created by Kristy Holm using home-made pinhole cameras. All other images are archived in the Europeana Collections at Creative Commons and are in the public domain. All are published online and labeled as free for reuse with modification.

Anne de Marcken is a writer and interdisciplinary artist. Her work includes hybrid fictions and realities, short and feature-length films, and site-specific installations. She is founding editor and publisher of The 3rd Thing.

Made in the USA
Middletown, DE
11 March 2024